. . . LIFELINES . . .

Communicating with Your Teen

...LIFELINES...

COMMUNICATING
WITH YOUR
TEEN

GREG & MICHAEL SMALLEY

Tyndale House Publishers, Inc.
WHEATON, ILLINOIS

Visit Tyndale's exciting Web site at www.tyndale.com

Designed by Ron Kaufmann

Published in association with the literary agency of Alive Communications, Inc., 7680 Goddard Street, Suite 200, Colorado Springs, CO 80920

Library of Congress Cataloging-in-Publication Data

Smalley, Greg.
  Communicating with your teen / Greg and Michael Smalley.
    p. cm.—(Life Lines)
Includes bibliographical references.
  ISBN 0-8423-6017-4 (sc)
  1. Parenting—Religious aspects—Christianity. 2. Parent and teenager—Religious aspects—Christianity. 3. Christian teenagers—Religious life. I. Smalley, Michael. II. Title.
BV4529 .S474 2003
248.8'45—dc21   2002152207

Printed in the United States of America

07 06 05 04 03
7   6   5   4   3   2   1

. . . ABOUT LIFE LINES . . .

The Life Lines series is designed for *real* people in *real life* situations. Written by published authors who are experts in their field, each book covers a different topic and includes:

- information you need, in a quick and easy-to-read format
- practical advice and encouragement from someone who's been there
- "life support"—hands-on tips to give you immediate help for the problems you're facing
- "healthy habits"—long-term strategies that will enrich your life
- inspiring Bible verses
- lists of additional resources—books, Web sites, videos, and seminars to keep you headed on the right path

Life Lines is a joint effort from Marriage Alive International and Smalley Relationship Center. Marriage Alive founders and directors David and Claudia Arp serve as general editors.

Whether you need assistance for an everyday situation, a life transition, or a crisis period, or you're just looking for a friend to come alongside you, Life Lines offers wise, compassionate counsel from someone who can help. This series will connect with you, inspire you, and give you tools that will change your life—for the better!

Titles in the series:
Life Lines: Connecting with Your Husband—Gary Smalley
Life Lines: Connecting with Your Wife—Barbara Rosberg

. . . CONTENTS . . .

Do you ever wonder . . .

- how that sweet, baby-powdered bundle of joy who couldn't stand to be apart from you has turned into a tall stranger who wants to hide out in his room rather than be anywhere near you?
- how you have suddenly changed from the parent who can comfort or fix anything into that person who "doesn't understand anything"?
- if all those early lessons in please-and-thank-you left any impression whatsoever?
- if you'll ever be able to fall asleep while your teenager is away from home—or behind the wheel?
- if you and your teenager will ever again have a normal, loving relationship?

If any of these ideas have crossed your mind or you ever lie awake at night worrying or praying over the decisions your teenager is making, welcome to the launch years!

The years when a teenager is approaching the age at which he'll leave home—whether to go away for more education, for a job, or just to move out on his own—are a time when both parents and teens struggle to find their way. Communication can be tough. Not only are your teens developing independence and logical thinking, they're also going through a major change in the way they see themselves. And you may be going through changes or stresses at the same time. There are many reasons why this time is so often fraught with conflict and miscommunication—and many of these reasons are quite natural! But there are also many ways to get ready for these years and to survive them with good grace, leaving the relationship between you and your young adult intact.

> These are tumultuous times for any family, but your family can ride out the storm with comfort and peace. Wisdom is available that you can wear like a good rain slicker, and positive actions can fit your lifestyle like good waterproof boots.

If ever there was a season when parents need to tap into every available source of wisdom, this is it! We have distilled some of the best advice out there for parents, and we're offering it here to you. As our foundation, we're depending on the ultimate source of wisdom, God's message to humankind—the Bible.

These are tumultuous times for any family, but in the same way you stay warm and dry within your

. . .

home while wind and rain beat outside, your family can ride out the emotional storms in comfort and peace. Wisdom is available that you can wear like a good rain slicker, and positive actions can fit your lifestyle like good waterproof boots. Talking to your teen doesn't have to be painful. You *can* learn to solve conflicts and communicate with openness and respect. How do we know? First, because we both survived our teenage years—with a good relationship with our parents intact. And second, because we both now counsel families and speak at conferences through the Smalley Relationship Center. We've seen these strategies work for family after family, and they can work for you too! We believe that with God's help, you can keep a calm mind and spirit as you launch your teen into the adult world.

WARNING: ROUGH WATERS AHEAD

All our parents wanted was some quality family time. But as teens, Michael and I wanted something different . . . *independence!* Which is what started the major conflict that fateful day on the island of Catalina. . . .

"Let's all go to the beach today!" our parents said excitedly. They were ready for some time with just the family—all of us together.

Being typical teenagers, we had no desire to hang out with the family. We wanted to explore some caves

. . .

we'd seen the previous day. "We don't want to hang out with you; it's too boring anyway!"

"It's too boring hanging out with you"—ever heard that one before? That's pretty much what started the Great Catalina Island Smalley Family Fight. We went round and round until our parents finally figured they would enjoy the day a lot more without two whining teenagers around. So we stormed off, little knowing that the day would hold not only basic family conflict but an actual struggle to survive!

We were snorkeling around the cliffs by the shore when we found a cave about the size of a large family room. At one end of the cave was an opening in the floor (about the size of a Jacuzzi) filled with water. We decided to explore the water hole with our underwater flashlights. The farther we went down the wider the hole got, branching off into several other smaller holes—one of which had light shining through. We figured that this hole must lead out into the ocean, which was on the other side of the cave.

I (Greg) took a big breath of air and swam down toward the small hole. As I maneuvered through the opening, I encountered a strong current. I could feel the tide pulling me as it went out and pushing me as it came back in. This should have been my first clue that it might not be such a good idea to go through this hole.

．．．

Nevertheless I pushed on. About ten yards into the hole, I came to a fork. Both tunnels looked alike and had the same amount of light shining through, so I quickly chose one. This tunnel headed straight up; I thought I was home free. I had already been in the cave for over a minute, and my lungs were starting to burn from a lack of oxygen. As I made my way up through the tunnel, a strong current pulled me along.

I had gone only a few yards in this direction when the area around me began to shrink. Quickly I realized that I wasn't going to fit through. I tried to back my way out, but the current was too strong—and it was pulling me toward the top. I had to wait until the tide started to come in before I could get out.

I was now starting to gasp violently for air, but when I got out of the tunnel I couldn't decide if I should try the other tunnel or go back the way I had come. Either way it looked about the same distance. However, when the tide went back out, the decision was out of my hands—I was sucked into the other tunnel. Panic took over my mind as I realized that if this tunnel did not lead to the surface, I would drown before I could make it back to the cave.

The speed at which I was now going through the tunnel caused me to scrape hard against the sides. I could feel deep gashes caused by the sharp coral, but being cut was the least of my worries. I now had to

． ． ．

fight my way through the returning tide. I imagined that this was what a salmon must feel like as he fights his way upstream. As hard as I was kicking my legs, it seemed as if I was making no progress. Struggling through the tunnel toward the light, all I could think about was that I didn't want to die like this. Finally, as the tide went out again, the water shot me through the tunnel and up to the surface. The noise of my inhaling must have sounded like the mating call of some strange mammal. But I was alive!

When I found my brother, still in the cave, he was crying. He thought I had died while trying to get through the cave. As I told him about the experience, my brother became amused. When I asked him what was so funny, he pointed out a big sign that was posted near the front of the entrance. The sign basically explained about the danger of trying to swim through the tunnels. It ended with "Under No Circumstances Is Anyone Allowed to Swim through the Tunnels!" How Michael and I didn't noticed the sign as we entered the cave I'll never understand.

That pushing-pulling, panicked state I experienced down in that tunnel is something like the experience of many parents who have teens. Sometimes the conflicts with these young adults leave both parent and child with emotional cuts and bruises (like the physical gouges I received from that coral!). Many par-

. . .

ents—and sometimes the teens too—are feeling exhausted by swimming hard against the current but seeing little progress.

Our hope is that we can put up a few red-flag warning signs for you, as parents, as you move through these years of launching your adolescent into adulthood. We want to give you direction so you can maneuver through the parent-and-teen conflicts, which often feel like a maze. We'll show you some practical communication solutions in these pages so that when you reach the end of this adolescent period in your family you won't be gasping for air, or nursing cuts and bruises. It's our goal to help your family emerge in a healthier condition.

In your relationship with your teenager, some conflict is a given—that's the bottom line! The good news is that you can use the conflict to build a better relationship, and not let it tear apart the love you share with your child.

In these pages we'll explain why conflict is a part of the relationship with your teen and help you see conflict as an opportunity to develop a strong and lasting relationship. We'll provide both immediate life support and then long-term help for creating healthier habits of dealing with anger and conflict with your adolescent, and of communicating with him or her.

Let's get started!

SPARKS ARE GONNA FLY!
The Reasons behind Parent-Teen Conflict

One mother we know is so resigned to the teenage argumentative response, she actually met her son at the door one day when she returned home from work and told him: "We're invited to the Stevens' for dinner. You've got thirty minutes to clean up and argue about it."

Conflict is inevitable in any relationship, but especially in the relationship between parents and teens. Since it's nearly impossible to avoid conflict in this stage, the wisest response is to learn to recognize why it occurs and seek to manage it positively. Take a look at some of the factors we've found that cause the most disagreements among parents and teens.

TEEN ISSUES

Developmental changes

Sometimes it feels as if teens actually enjoy arguing with authority! It's important for parents to recognize that it's natural for conflict to increase during adolescence. As your child hits the teenage years, a very important developmental change occurs involving his or her intellectual abilities. Before your son reached adolescence, there were times when he thought you, his parents, knew everything. He was amazed at the seemingly endless amount of knowledge you possessed, and he assumed you could handle any situation. This is because younger children have difficulty looking at the bigger picture; instead, they focus on literal or concrete ideas. They also have limited experience with the world and find it difficult to judge logical consistency. This is why it's easy for most young kids to believe in Santa Claus. Even though it's clearly not logical to believe that one man could visit every house in the world in one night, traveling in a sleigh pulled by flying reindeer, young children believe that he does. Why? They have concrete proof that he exists—presents!

When kids reach adolescence, however, parents say good-bye to the days of literal meaning and difficulty with logic. A teen's ability to reason and grapple with abstract ideas pushes him to think and create solutions and resolutions independently. Does it ever feel like your teenage daughter thinks she knows everything? At this age, most teenagers feel the need to challenge authority or established experts. They don't want to take anyone's word for it; they want to find answers for themselves. The result? Your child no longer believes every word you say just because you said it.

Yet just because your teen is developing the ability to think and reason in the abstract doesn't mean he or she is always going to exercise high logical ability. In fact, most parents find it pretty frustrating if they try to use logic when arguing with their teens. Jean Piaget, a pioneer and expert in the area of cognitive development, discovered that a teenager's thoughts

---

THE TOP TEN CONFLICTS BETWEEN PARENTS AND TEENAGERS

We interviewed 2,000 parents to ascertain the conflicts they most often experienced with their teens. The following are the top ten trigger points that set off sparks:

- TV/video games
- Talking/communicating
- Chores
- Cleaning
- Taking care of family property
- Discipline: setting limits, enforcing rules, being too lenient
- Spending time with family
- Siblings
- The way the teenager speaks to parents
- Teenager not telling parents how he feels or thinks

are usually quite idealistic. She may be able to think about the future and its endless possibilities, but she still has trouble thinking in practical terms. Sometimes a teen's overly optimistic outlook on the future causes trouble because he or she doesn't yet understand the many obstacles or difficulties that must be overcome to reach these future goals. In an attempt to help their teen be more realistic, parents sometimes go overboard with caution, and teens perceive this concern as criticism.

> Teens have new abilities and gifts and can't wait to try them out. There probably isn't a better "practice field" for experimental arguing than at home with you.

In addition to idealistic thinking, teens are beginning to develop the mental capacity for problem solving. They're learning to detect the logical consistency or inconsistency in a set of statements, especially statements made by authority figures. In other words, you can no longer expect your child to accept that "there are starving children in Africa who would love it" as a reasonable reason for eating his broccoli.

These physiological changes in your teen's brain will affect your disagreements with him. If it seems like every time you bring up a topic, your teen wants to argue about it, it's probably because of these developmental changes. Arguing with you doesn't necessarily mean that your teen loves to terrorize you or that you two have a shaky relationship. Instead of being discouraged, try thinking of your adolescent's new mental abilities as a Christmas present. When you first unwrap a present, you're filled with excitement and want to use your new gift all the time. It's the same for teenagers. They have new abilities and gifts and can't wait to try them out. They probably won't find a better "practice field" for experimental arguing than at home with the family. Teenagers need to be able to utilize these new idealistic and logical abilities.

Social changes

Teen-parent fights have a lot of common triggers. Take a look at the sidebar on page 3 for some specific ones. But a number of underlying social and behavioral issues can also be factors in conflict:

- **Privacy.** Teenagers usually develop an intense desire for privacy. Sometimes young people who were never overly shy as children become reluctant to reveal themselves, their feelings, and their ideas once they reach the teen years. This change, which necessarily creates distance in the teen-parent relationship, is often difficult for both parents and adolescents to negotiate. You may feel hurt that your child no longer confides in you; your teen may feel upset by the distance even as she insists upon it. This results in—what else?—conflict.

- **Risky behavior.** Another source of friction may develop as teens begin to engage in rebellious, show-offy, or risk-taking behaviors—and that drives the concerned parent completely crazy! Perhaps the teen drives fast or recklessly. Perhaps he stops studying or experiments with alcohol, drugs, or premarital sex. Teens often have an unrealistic "it can't happen to me" attitude that rejects the notion of danger or resists the long-term view of these often self-destructive activities.
- **Friendships.** It's common for teens to value their friends—and the advice and input they receive from friends—more than their parents during adolescence. Parents and family, who are forced to take a backseat to these favored relationships, may feel rejected. Peer pressure becomes an issue, as "the group" exerts an almost irresistible influence on your child.
- **Dating.** Young people also begin to pull away from their families more as they begin to date, finding friends of the opposite sex in whom to confide and on whom to depend.
- **Working.** The potential for conflict increases when your young person steps out into the world of employment—a world complete with a busy

•   •   •

schedule that can be difficult to merge with the family or school schedule and an income that may not necessarily be spent wisely or well.

- **Fads and fashions.** As young people express their individuality by making fashion or being "in style" a priority, new areas of conflict often emerge. Parents may disagree with teens spending money on fad clothing or styles that are disagreeable to them. Sometimes teens want to dress in a way that's sexy without understanding the dangers associated with that choice. They also tend to be excessively focused on their looks, and they may give this aspect of their personhood too much importance—either capitalizing on good looks or despairing over average ones. Both girls and guys may struggle with body image and eating disorders.

In short, teens are experiencing more choices than they ever have before, and the newfound freedom can be both exhilarating and frightening.

Most tension between parents and teens grows out of the young person's movement toward becoming an individual separate from the family group. Generally, the young person's longing for more autonomy— "I'm in charge of me"—smacks up against what you, the parents, know he or she is really ready for. As you struggle to find the balance between how much re-sponsibility can be shifted to the teen and which areas of authority need to remain in your domain, you may begin to feel as if you're always arguing with your child. But take heart. There is a way to navigate these choppy waters and reach a solution everyone can live with.

PARENTS' ISSUES

While teens are changing, so are you, Mom and Dad. You may find that the atmosphere of conflict in the home is taking its toll on your marriage too. It's typi-cal for marital satisfaction to dip during these years of parenting teens.

Midlife issues

Adolescence arrives at a rather inconvenient time for some parents. It comes when many middle-aged par-ents are asking themselves: *Who am I, what have I accomplished, where am I now, and what does the future hold for me?* In some ways, midlife parallels adolescence.[1]

Some women look toward the empty-nest future and realize they may want to pursue more education or a different job—especially if they've put careers on hold in order to spend years raising their families. Other parents find themselves doing work in a field that hasn't brought them much personal satisfaction, yet they may feel trapped by financial obligations to their family. Many people in the midlife years look for drastic changes—in education, hobbies, cars, and so on. If this sounds like you, consider talking to a

---

PARENTING ON YOUR OWN

If you're a single parent of a teenager, you don't need anyone to tell you that you're facing some extra challenges. Here are a few tips to encourage you in your task:

- **Look for support.** Every parent needs a sounding board— someone with whom he or she can discuss tough issues like discipline, homework, and TV limits. Cultivate relationships with other parents who can fill this void in your life. Maybe it's a couple at church who has children about the same age as yours, or possibly it's an older man or woman who has been there and can share wisdom. Don't be afraid to ask for help when you need it.

- **Create new traditions.** It's inevitable that kids will compare the way things are now to the way things used to be. While some old traditions are worth maintaining, sometimes it's best to make a break from the past. Sit down with your kids and brainstorm some creative new ideas. Maybe you'll want to implement Saturday-morning breakfast in bed, or a special family movie night once a month.

- **Be honest but reassuring.** If you've gone through a divorce or the death of a spouse, your kids need to know that some things are different now. Maybe they'll have to move to a different neighborhood or quit piano lessons. Maybe they won't be able to have Saturday-morning breakfast with Dad. Talk to them about these changes, but be upfront about the things that will stay the same: your love for them, their identity as your children, God's care.

counselor and looking for a way to make positive changes. If you're interested in a new career, check out the career section of your library or local bookstore. Several books are available that will help you evaluate your interests and skills.

> **Not only is life dramatically changing for the adolescent, but there are important adjustments for the parents and the family as well.**

Furthermore, many parents experience an "authority crisis." They feel their authority is being threatened as the teen questions their values and rules, which is part of the process of individuation. Parents may also begin to question themselves.[2] If they made mistakes in their own adolescence, such as experimenting with drugs and alcohol or having a child out of wedlock, they may become increasingly frightened and try to control their teen's behavior to make sure history doesn't repeat itself.

Another stress affecting parents at this time is the increase in the family's financial burden. Teens have more expensive activities and pastimes, and car insurance for teen drivers is costly. College is now in the not so distant future, and many parents may be forced to do some fast figuring—and sometimes some take on side jobs—in order to make college a possibility for their children. In families where teens are required to contribute to car-insurance payments or college savings funds, parents may find that motivating their teens is anotheer source of stress.

Other personal stresses may affect the adults. Perhaps their own physical attractiveness is in decline, which can be hard on some people. What's worse, they may be dealing with more health and physical concerns. Many parents are extraordinarily busy, driving their teens to and from activities while trying to work at home or on the road. Some parents must join the "sandwich generation" and care for their own elderly parents as well as their children.

A matter of style

No matter what your parenting style, these teen years can be tough. Adults who struggle with low self-esteem, or parents who have until now enjoyed a good relationship with their children, may be hurt by their adolescent's preference for outside input and friendships. Parents who have been more controlling or authoritarian will find that trying to exert control at this stage of the game usually leads to more conflict with their teens, who struggle even harder for independence. And parents with rigid or unrealistic expectations for their kids will find these years especially difficult. Teens who are struggling to discover who they are and what they want out of life may revolt against having to measure up to anyone else's standards.

. . .

FAMILY ISSUES

Family styles and the changes that take place during these tumultuous years can also contribute to the background causes of conflict. Family relationships undergo a transformation when children reach adolescence. Parents and teens spend less time together during adolescence than earlier in life.[3] Many of the interaction patterns that were appropriate for parents and their preschool- or elementary-school-age children are no longer appropriate for interactions between parents and soon-to-be-adult offspring.[4] A teen who is bent on autonomy will likely spot these patterns and rebel against them before the parent—who can't quite believe his or her child is growing up—does.

The organization of the family also plays a part. Has there been a divorce, resulting in single-parent home life or stepfamily situations? Split families can have more financial pressure and less geographic mobility, and it is more likely that the mother will have to work outside the home. Families recovering from divorce or adjusting to a blended situation must deal with complex issues, such as trying to merge parenting styles, deal with new sibling relationships, and cope with loss and change. All of these add to tension in the home. (For help with these tough issues, check out the titles listed in the resource section at the back of this book.)

. . .

Differences in the personality types in the family members often become more noticeable and pronounced as teens "come into their own." Differences that used to be easily managed or accepted may shift into more marked opposition. A picky eater may

---

THE BRADY BUNCH?

Okay, so life as a blended family may not be quite as harmonious and fun as it used to look on *The Brady Bunch*—especially if you have teenagers. Melding two families together takes time, careful planning, and lots of effort. How do you do it?

- **Don't compete.** Most kids in a blended family have two sets of parents—and that can set the stage for lots of competition. Just say no! Focus on the relationship with your children, not on how you compare with the "other" mom or dad.

- **Set clear rules—and stick to them.** No two families are exactly alike, so it's inevitable that you'll encounter different expectations. Sit down together as a *new* family and hash out some rules: for household chores, for curfew, for homework, for conflict resolution, for discipline. Teens who suspect favoritism will be less likely to wail "It's not fair!" if it's clear that *all* the kids follow the same rules.

- **Back each other up.** How many times have you heard that parents shouldn't disagree on discipline in front of the kids? That can become a lot harder when you're watching your spouse punish *your* child. But be careful. When you side with your kids over your spouse, you're undermining his or her authority and setting the stage for more conflict down the road.

- **Be patient.** Putting two separate families into one household is a major change. Recognize that you *and* your kids need time to adjust. Expect that things won't always go smoothly, and take the time to celebrate all the little milestones you pass.

become a strict vegetarian when she becomes a teenager and turn every family meal into a diatribe against meat eaters. A child who has always been quiet by nature may become even more quiet and withdrawn during the teen years, especially if his parents or siblings are more extroverted. Sibling rivalry often intensifies as one child or another gets more attention, even if that attention is negative.

These years change the family's emotional connections. Parents and teens are more emotionally distant, often separated by conflicts of morals and values. As your teen attempts to find his own set of values, it will often seem as if he's rejecting everything you've taught him about right and wrong. Don't worry. This is normal. In order to build a strong moral foundation for his life, your child needs to understand *why* he believes what he believes. Most parents find that their children do return to what they've been taught as they move into adulthood.

KNOWLEDGE IS POWER

With the teen's developmental and social changes, parents' midlife issues, and questions about the family's style, it's no wonder this period can be fraught with tension! Not only is life dramatically changing for the adolescent, but there are important adjustments for the parents and the family as well.

. . .

Is there any help for this situation? Of course. Once you understand some of the reasons behind the conflicts you experience with your teen, you'll be better equipped to handle the problems. It's not that your teenage son or daughter actually enjoys arguing with you, or that your family is dysfunctional or unhealthy because conflict exists. Instead, you need to realize that you're all going through significant changes.

As a parent, you might be feeling somewhat hopeless and helpless in response to this challenging and adjustment-filled period called adolescence. However, before you get too discouraged, remember that conflict is normal and natural in close relationships. Conflict is a part of both breaking down barriers and sharing feelings and needs. But the best news of all is that conflict is loaded with opportunity. *Conflict as opportunity . . . impossible!* you might be thinking. But in the next chapter we'll show you that great opportunity exists if you learn how to better manage conflict with your teens.

> *May God, who gives this patience and encouragement, help you live in complete harmony with each other— each with the attitude of Christ Jesus toward the other. Then all of you can join together with one voice, giving praise and glory to God, the Father of our Lord Jesus Christ.*
>
> ROMANS 15:5-6

CONFLICT AS OPPORTUNITY

Conflict isn't fun—and it's rarely pretty. So it's no wonder most of us dislike it and try to avoid it whenever possible. And it's perfectly normal for parents to want to avoid conflicts with their teens. Because we love our teens so much and our relationships may already be tenuous, we dread the possibility of weakening these already fragile relationships.

But conflict is inevitable. It's a natural part of all relationships, healthy or unhealthy. All relationships—with our teenagers, colleagues, friends, extended family, church acquaintances, or neighbors—will experience conflict because people differ so greatly as individuals. And we should value those differences!

Because we're different in personality, gender, opinions, concerns, and expectations, it's only natural that we disagree.

So don't be alarmed as you begin to experience disputes and disagreements with your teenager. Rather than worry about when and if conflict will occur, instead determine now how you'll handle any conflict when it does crop up.

> The new goal is not to eliminate disagreements, but to reach the other side together, with a closer bond between you and your child.

Conflict is actually a valuable crossroads—a point of growth in your relationship with your teen. This may be a major paradigm shift for some of you, especially if you're been in the habit of avoiding conflict altogether. But we want you to see conflict as an opportunity to deepen your connection with your teen, not as a threat that will damage your relationship.

So the new goal is not to eliminate disagreements, but to reach the other side together, with a closer bond between you and your child. Your relationship is changing, certainly; you can either use this time to grow together or grow apart. The way you handle the critical interactions and conflict will be a key tool in improving your relationship. It is possible to have a stronger relationship if you, as the parent, get a good handle on the conflict and learn to manage it rather than letting *it* control *you*.

. . .

Let's explore the opportunities conflict provides! Here are five specific areas.

CONNECT WITH YOUR TEEN

Conflicts, if handled in a healthy manner, have the potential to draw you and your teen closer to each other. In fact, disagreements are a necessary part of the process of drawing near to loved ones! That's not to say that you should go about "itching for a fight"— looking for conflict just so you can enjoy a deeper connection. No way! But when arguments occur, they can bring benefits, if you manage them properly.

In the final book of the Chronicles of Narnia series, *The Last Battle,* C. S. Lewis describes a scene in which the characters face a battle to end all battles. They try in vain to escape being thrown into a stable that some people claim holds a life-threatening creature. But once they are through that doorway, they discover that "in reality they stood on grass, the deep blue sky was overhead, and the air which blew gently on their faces was that of a day in early summer."[5] Walking through that door had taken them to a heavenly kingdom. And once there, they could continue to go "further up and further in," making increasingly awesome, wonderful, new discoveries that they couldn't have fathomed before they walked through that seemingly threatening door.

Conflict with your teen can be like that threatening door in those final pages of *The Last Battle*. It looks like—it even *feels* like—conflict is going to be a terrifying monster, out of control. Instead, as you open the door to connecting with your teen—never closing it, slamming it, or locking it—you'll find that it leads to a path of understanding, of mutual sharing, and lasting relationship. When you can see or imagine the "green grass and blue sky" through that doorway of conflict, it takes some of the fear away. You don't need to be afraid of conflict when disagreements become the agent that moves your relationship forward.

Deeper connection is the treasure buried in conflict. If things are very difficult in your family just now and you feel overwhelmed by the amount and extent of negative interactions between you and your teen, the idea that conflict is healthy may sound like a cruel joke to you. But conflict management is the lifeblood of a relationship. Relationships live or die by their arguments, by the positive or negative way grievances are aired. The difference lies in whether your arguments simply escalate the family

> **The most important piece of clothing you must wear is love. Love is what binds us all together in perfect harmony. And let the peace that comes from Christ rule in your hearts. For as members of one body you are all called to live in peace. And always be thankful.**
>
> COLOSSIANS 3:14-15

. . .

tension or lead eventually to feelings of resolution.[6] We hope to help you get those arguments moving in the right direction.

VALIDATE YOUR TEEN

At a marriage seminar we lead every month, we asked the adults: "What do you wish your parents had done differently during times of conflict when you were a teenager?" Can you guess what the top two answers were?

1. Adults wished their parents would have listened more.
2. Adults wished they could have talked more about their feelings.

We also asked these adults, "Now as parents, which things most frustrate you about your teenagers?" Amazingly, the exact things they wished their parents would have done differently are the things they get upset about with their teens.

1. Teens don't talk about how they feel.
2. Teens don't always listen.

Communication, listening, and sharing feelings are at the heart of validation. The amazing truth about conflict is that, if used correctly, it allows you to validate your teenagers by listening to them and understanding them. Validation simply means that you value a person's opinions, ideas, concerns, needs, and feelings. It doesn't mean that you agree with what they're saying but you give them a sense that you really "get" them. During a conflict, either you can force your teen to agree with your position or you can provide him with an experience of being heard and understood. The latter option is validation. When you validate someone, you don't argue about what he's saying; instead, you seek first to understand. If you are able to validate your son, he should walk away with a very clear message: "Mom thinks my opinions, needs, and feelings are valuable." What a tremendous gift!

UNDERSTAND YOUR TEEN

Conflict resolution begins with *listening*—not with searching for solutions. Whenever we're in a serious conversation with someone, it can be very tempting to focus on finding a solution to the problem. This is especially true for men. Teens often complain that their dads don't pay enough attention to what they're saying because they're too busy offering solutions or "fixing" the problem. It's important that parents— fathers *and* mothers—cultivate the practice of listen-

ing first and then looking for ways to resolve problems or conflicts.

What kinds of things should you be listening for as
you talk with your teen?

1. Needs and feelings
2. Worries and anxieties
3. Feelings of loneliness
4. Hopes and dreams
5. Struggles and frustrations

MODEL HEALTHY CONFLICT RESOLUTION

One of the skills your teens will need most if they
hope to be successful in their relationships is the ability to resolve conflicts. The primary place your children will learn about conflict resolution is at home.
You can teach them all they need to know about this
important skill, because what they learn will be critical in the future as they begin to develop their own
relationships with others.

We're not saying that you should always argue or
fight with your spouse in front of the kids so that
they learn how to resolve conflicts. There are many
topics and issues that are extremely inappropriate to
discuss with children present—your sex life and disciplining your kids are two of the most obvious! Also,
if the conversation is extremely heated or emotional,

.   .   .

it's best to continue it behind closed doors. On the other hand, it's perfectly acceptable to discuss minor disagreements in front of your children. In doing so, you can model healthy tactics. They can listen in as you figure out household responsibilities or discuss your budget. It's important that your teens hear you validating your spouse, to see that you listen to one another and attempt to understand the other's position. It's especially critical for them to see the tools you use that will lead to win/win solutions.

When Michael and I were growing up, many times our parents argued about money. We knew they were in disagreement, but we had the privilege of seeing them work through the conflict in a reasonably healthy manner. The bottom line was that they used appropriate discretion regarding the issue. In other instances, they let us know they'd had a disagreement but worked it out, without offering inappropriate details like how Dad had blown the budget or what the remaining checking account balance was. You might try sharing the process with your kids— how you worked out your disagreement—rather than focusing on the specifics of the conflict.

Your goal in these years of parenting a teen is to launch your teenager into successful adulthood. Think how good conflict-management skills will help your child in dorm-room situations or sticky issues with professors at college; with the everyday "bumps in the road" at work with employers and coworkers; with relationships within the church family; and with his or her future spouse and children. You give your child an incredible gift when you send him or her into adult life with the richness of conflict-management skills!

MOVE TOWARD HEALTHY INDEPENDENCE

Children are dependent upon their parents for emotional, intellectual, and physical needs. During adolescence, however, teens must begin to separate from their parents. But much like a baby bird needs some forceful "persuading," teenagers sometimes need some urging to leave the nest as well. Think about it: Why would a teen ever leave home if things were harmonious and peaceful? Well, okay, most teens would eventually reach a point where they wanted their own space. But we believe that conflict at home during the adolescent years is necessary so the teen moves toward separation and individuation.

> *Hold to the truth in love, becoming more and more in every way like Christ, who is the head of his body, the church.*
>
> EPHESIANS 4:15

This is yet another reason why conflict is so valuable for your teen. When your teenager disagrees with you, trying out his own ideas and opinions, that means he *has* his own ideas and opinions. Isn't that great? Wasn't that part of the goal?

. . .

Even if it's tough for you, in your maturity, to handle the specific ideas and opinions your teen is expressing, it's possible to see the growth of independence in the fact that he's trying on adult roles. As you handle those conflicting ideas and opinions well, you'll be better equipped to hang on to your relationship. That allows you to have future influence in shaping that young individual's ideas and opinions (which, hopefully, will keep on growing up, just like he is!).

In the next chapter we'll take a look at what can happen when we don't manage conflict well. Then we'll give you some quick tips to make sure you *do* manage conflict the right way.

...3...

WHEN CONFLICT DOESN'T GO YOUR WAY

The good news: Your conflicts can be put to work to improve your relationship with your teen. The bad news: Poorly managed conflict can damage your relationship. But don't be discouraged. Understanding the negative possibilities is the first step toward getting motivated to do better during your disagreements with your teen.

When conflict is not handled in a healthy manner, a number of negative things can occur. In this chapter, we'll talk about four of them: withdrawal, escalation, belittling, and exaggerated or false ideas.

．　．　．

Withdrawal

Have you ever been in the middle of a disagreement
with your teen when one of you completely shuts the
other out? "I'm not talking about this anymore!" "End
of discussion! If you bring this up again, I'm leaving!"
Doors slam and feelings are hurt.

So much for feelings of resolution—or for the feelings of achievement that come when two people work
their way through a disagreement. Withdrawal closes
the door to all the relationship opportunities we've
been talking about.

Escalation

Think of escalation as a kind of spiraling volley that
moves an argument in uglier and uglier directions.

When one person becomes defensive or
insistently tries to win, it's easy to start
shouting, blaming each other, using de-
grading names, and so forth. You'll recognize some signs of escalation in the
overuse of the word *you*: "Don't you ac-
cuse me!" "You always—." "You
never—." "You're just mean/stupid/
selfish." There's a kind of crazy one-up-
manship going on here, as if the two of you need to
best each other in a match of temper or intensity.

Escalation will take your relationship in a direction

> Unless you're a
> superhuman
> parent, it's likely
> that some of these
> "downsides"
> of conflict have
> crept into your
> conflict style.

···

away from closeness and connection by bringing in an element of competition and allowing negative emotions to spiral out of control.

Belittling

When a conflict escalates, it's a short stretch to belittling. It's not long before you start accusing each other of being stupid or inferior. This is some sort of defensive move to make yourself feel better than or superior to your opponent in conflict. Ever heard statements like these in your arguments? "That's the dumbest thing I've ever heard!" "When will you ever get it right?" "You've been thinking from the wrong part of your body." "No wonder you get poor grades." "I wouldn't want to go out with you either!"

If your much-loved child suddenly turns into an opponent to attack, things have strayed a long way from the kind of conflict-management that validates and seeks mutual resolution.

Exaggerated or false ideas

In the heat of conflict, it's easy to develop exaggerated or false beliefs about your teen. For example, it might feel to you or him that one of you is *purposely* trying to ruin or weaken the relationship, although that's rarely true. Heard statements like these? "You always want to be around your friends. You don't care about me." Or, "You don't even try to understand where I'm coming from. You'd try if you really cared." These negative beliefs are powerful because they affect how each of us perceives and interprets what the other does! Those perceptions are often more pivotal in shaping our relationship—and our level of satisfaction in the relationship—than the realities are.

Humans tend to see and hear what they want to see and hear about another person, even if it isn't true. In other words, what you believe about another person—positive or negative—clouds your perspective about that person. And soon, you'll find evidence to support what you believe in everything that person does or says. If you think your teen isn't very smart or is awkward in social situations, you'll begin to focus only on the negative behavior that supports that image. It doesn't matter what reality is; you will view it from the lens of your beliefs about your child. It's the same thing that Paul wrote about in Romans 14:14: "To him who considers anything to be unclean, to him it is unclean" (NKJV).

Ever heard of the "self-fulfilling prophecy"? The idea is that, once you've got an idea in your head, you'll begin to look for and notice behaviors that reinforce that thought. Once you've negatively "framed" your teen in your mind—as only average in intelligence, for example—you'll tend to treat him as if he's

• • •

not very smart. That effectively shuts the door on positive reinforcements. People tend to live up to our beliefs about them (thus, the self-fulfilling prophecy). When negative thinking consistently invades your relationship, it produces an environment of hopelessness and demoralization. The teen who's been negatively framed is robbed of motivation and action.

PREVENTING FUTURE PROBLEMS

When families manage their conflicts poorly, more trouble follows. Maybe your teen loses respect for your advice and instead becomes constantly critical of your words and actions. Maybe your daughter develops an argumentative attitude all the time—and not just with you. Or maybe your son, in anger and hurt, intentionally seeks out friends who are the opposite of the ones you'd choose for him. Maybe her language becomes increasingly disrespectful or foul. Maybe his facial expressions begin to reflect constant anger or even violence. Sometimes your kids will purposely avoid you, or at least turn their backs on you. Other times, they withhold affection, along with any expression of caring feelings. Sometimes teens begin to "medicate" their emotional pain with sex, alcohol, or drugs.

Unless you're a superhuman parent, it's likely that some of these downsides of conflict have crept into

. . .

your conflict style. But now that you've seen how conflict can bring opportunities for improving your relationship with your teen, you can begin immediately to handle conflicts in a more productive way. In the next chapter we'll look at some tangible ways you can do just that.

4

LIFE SUPPORT: IMMEDIATE RELATIONSHIP REPAIR

Perhaps you feel you're about to "lose it" or maybe you've already lost it with your teenager. Maybe you don't even know how to repair the relationship when your teen says that he hates you. Perhaps communication is awkward—or nonexistent. If you're in the middle of tremendous conflict with your teenager, don't panic! There's hope. There are steps you can take right away to dramatically decrease your fear and increase your chances of reconnecting with your teenager. Even if you already have a good relationship with your teen but want to make it better, these tips will help.

SEEK FORGIVENESS

The very first thing you need to do to combat the negative outcomes of poorly managed conflict is to seek forgiveness.

Ever heard the story of the monkey and the lion? "That's incredible, having a monkey and a lion together in the same cage," said the guest at a local zoo. "How do they get along?" "Pretty well, for the most part," answered the zookeeper. "Once in a while they have a disagreement, and we have to get a new monkey."

Perhaps your teenager feels like one of those monkeys—that when clashes come, he's sure to be the casualty. Your teenager may feel that each time you get into a disagreement, you come down on him like a strong lion. Clashes like these can leave a young person feeling wounded, as if his spirit has been "killed."

If this is the turn your conflicts have taken, it's

THE TRUTH ABOUT ANGER

- Anger is an intense emotional reaction that sometimes remains largely unexpressed and kept inside and at other times is directly expressed in outward behavior.
- Anger is one of many God-given emotions and is a natural and normal response to a variety of life's situations and stresses.
- Anger is a secondary emotion that is usually experienced in response to a primary emotion such as hurt, frustration, or fear.
- Anger can be a signal that we are being hurt, that our rights are being violated, that our needs or wants are being ignored.

very possible that your adolescent is dealing with unresolved anger. And research indicates that anger is physically, emotionally, and relationally damaging to teenagers. As parents, you must be persistent in helping your children deal constructively with their anger. How? By making sure your children feel comfortable approaching you and expressing their feelings. By watching your words and making sure you're not belittling your teen but building him up. By acknowledging your own mistakes and handling them with maturity.

So how should you seek forgiveness from your teen? There are three steps.

1. Take full responsibility for your actions. It doesn't help to point out your teenager's mistakes when you are seeking forgiveness. All that does is invalidate his feelings and lessen the power of forgiveness (not to mention reopen the hurts that caused his anger in the first place). If your teenager needs to seek your forgiveness, let him

Children, obey your parents because you belong to the Lord, for this is the right thing to do. "Honor your father and mother." This is the first of the Ten Commandments that ends with a promise. And this is the promise: If you honor your father and mother, "you will live a long life, full of blessing." And now a word to you fathers. Don't make your children angry by the way you treat them. Rather, bring them up with the discipline and instruction approved by the Lord.
EPHESIANS 6:1-4

figure that out and come to you on his own. It would mean more to you in the long run anyway.

Avoid placing blame or making excuses. Adding either of these two elements is like pouring salt on an open wound. If you feel the need to blame or make excuses, take a step back until your heart is more ready.

2. Be soft when approaching your teenager. Forgiveness loses its luster when requested with a harsh voice. Ask your teen if she is ready to talk yet, especially if the wounds inflicted are deep. Most importantly, be sincere with your softness. Authentic vulnerability gives your teenagers the chance for complete healing. It offers them a safe environment

---

MISMANAGED ANGER CAN BE HAZARDOUS TO YOUR HEALTH

Anger can lead to . . .

- Stress
- Burnout
- Physical illness
- Higher cholesterol levels
- Premature death—angry people are three times more likely to die prematurely than those who vent frustrations
- Suicide
- Constricted blood vessels
- Increased heart rate and blood pressure
- Destruction of heart muscle
- Depression
- Anxiety

---

in which to share their struggles and even to confront you when needed.

3. Ask specifically how you have hurt your teen. This allows your young adult to share his feelings—a skill that he'll certainly need throughout his adult life. If your teen isn't willing to share, don't push the subject. Sometimes you can help your teenager understand himself better by asking more specific questions about how he feels. The important thing is to not push or degrade your teen if he doesn't want to open up right away. Not sharing can mean that he isn't ready, that the hurt is still very strong, or that he doesn't feel safe enough to share. What this step does most is validate his pain—that is, acknowledge that his feelings are real and important and worth spending time on. This is a great way to release anger and hurt feelings.

HEALTHY ANGER MANAGEMENT

- Acknowledge that you are angry.
- Take a time-out and remove yourself from whatever is triggering the anger (e.g., talk to another person, take a walk, pray, watch TV).
- Take responsibility for your anger. No one makes you feel anything; it's your choice how you respond to others.
- Consider the causes. Was it fear, hurt, or frustration?
- Choose to respond in a healthy way.

. . .

What if your teen refuses to forgive? If you have followed these three steps and your teen still refuses to forgive you, there are several possible reasons why. Perhaps the offense was deeper than you realized or she wants to see your behavior change first. Perhaps she is still hurt by past offenses. Whatever the reason, the best thing is to be patient with your teen. No matter how she responds, never drop the issue altogether simply because she isn't ready to forgive you. Let the situation cool off for a while, then come back and repeat the three steps.

> **Parents must persistently help their children to deal constructively with their anger.**

Seeking forgiveness is a great first step in reconnecting with your teen. The step we'll cover in the next chapter is finding out what your teen needs from you—by asking one simple question.

5

LIFE SUPPORT: ASKING THE
$64,000 QUESTION

Did you know that one question can instantly improve your relationship with your teen? You're probably thinking, *Right! That sounds way too good to be true!* But it's true—something so important can be so simple. The key is this: Ask your teenager what specific things you can do to improve your relationship.

We've seen this truth played out many times in our counseling practice. The Petersons (not their real names) are a good example. Kathi Peterson came into our office with her parents, tears streaming down her face. It was clear that she was very angry. Mr. and Mrs. Peterson looked worried and defeated. It seemed like just yesterday that they understood exactly what their little girl needed from them. But now, as a teenager, Kathi seemed distant. They didn't feel as if they really understood her or what she wanted anymore.

Were they going to lose her? It was a terrifying thought. But at the rate they were going, they would surely lose their daughter if something didn't change.

Many parents of teenagers face these same kinds of questions and fears. You may find that what once worked for your teenager when she was younger no longer seems to be effective. What can you do as parents to understand what your teenagers need during this confusing period?

> The more you dwell on the problem and who's to blame, the faster and deeper you sink. But solutions are like a rope tied to a tree. They provide the means to change.

YOUR TEEN: A BUILT-IN RESOURCE

One of the greatest things you can do is discover your teen's built-in parenting manual. Many parents fail to realize that they have one of the world's greatest relational instructors living right under their own roof: their teenager! Teenagers have a natural insight into what they need from their parents and others to build strong relationships. In other words, most family members—if asked—could list the specific things they need from others in order to feel loved. Their list might include: time with friends, privacy, ways to

· · ·

earn trust, encouraging words from their parents, or the occasional use of the family car.

The key is that each individual has different needs and desires that help validate him or her in any strong relationship. So each person is a gold mine of relational information. As parents, we need to learn how to tap into this built-in knowledge.

How? First, *determine the type of relationship your teenager wants to have with you.* By using a scale from zero to ten, with zero being terrible and ten being a great relationship, ask your teenager where he would like your relationship to be. When the Petersons asked Kathi, she hesitantly said a nine or a ten. "After all," she explained, "I'm tired of living in misery!"

Next, *evaluate where the relationship is currently.* "On a scale from zero to ten," Kathi's parents asked, "overall, where would you rate our relationship today?"

"It's at a one!" Kathi said with hesitation. Although painful to hear, Mr. and Mrs. Peterson now had a clear picture of what they were facing.

When you ask your teenagers this question, don't be discouraged if they rate your relationship negatively.

FINISH THIS STATEMENT

Have your teen fill in the blank: "I feel loved or cared for when you _____."

Be sure to write down the responses so you don't forget.

Be sure to give them the necessary time to share why they rated the relationship the way they did. Each response can provide valuable information, so listen carefully.

The next question, however, is the crucial one. This question can potentially flip open the pages to your teen's built-in parenting manual: *As you consider our relationship, what are some specific things we can do over the next week that would move us closer to a ten?*

As Kathi answered this question, her parents hung on her every word. As she talked, she provided them with the exact things she needed to improve their relationship. It was a miracle!

SOLUTIONS INSTEAD OF PROBLEMS

The power of this last question is that it changes the focus of the relationship. Rather than feeling overwhelmed because you're focusing on all the problems, you begin focusing on solutions. You probably already know that being in the middle of a family conflict can feel like being stuck in quicksand. The more you dwell on the problem and who's to blame, the faster and deeper you sink. But solutions are like a rope tied to a tree. They keep the relationship from sinking hopelessly by providing the means to change.

As your teens begin to answer these three questions, remember that they may be reluctant at first.

Kathi did not believe that her parents really wanted to listen to her. Your teens might have similar fears. It's crucial to patiently give them the time necessary to talk. Constantly reassure them that the relationship is secure, no matter what is said or how things are rated. If your child feels secure in your love, she'll be more willing to provide helpful specifics that can strengthen the relationship God has given you.

Although Kathi and her parents knew that problems would surface again, they also felt more confident after their discussion because they could deal with those problems head-on.

What would happen if you asked your teenager the $64,000 question? Ask it, and find out!

6

LIFE SUPPORT: TAKE A TIME-OUT

Dick Vitale, the sports announcer for ESPN, has a common refrain: "Take a time-out, baby!" We doubt he ever thought he'd be used to help parents in conflict with their teenagers. However, this idea of taking a time-out is critical to decreasing tension in your home immediately, especially if you feel the need to defuse an emotional time bomb.

We're going to get into greater detail about taking time-outs when we talk about loving communication in the chapters to come. But as an immediate "life-support" kind of intervention, a time-out can be a real lifesaver.

When the sparks fly and conflict erupts between

you and your teenager, don't allow things to spiral out of control. Cut the huge bursts of anger short with a time-out.

We encourage you to actually say, "Whoa, this is getting way out of hand. Let's call a time-out and take a break for a while." A time-out stops the conflict immediately and allows both parties to calm down and collect their emotions.

Dr. John Gottman is a leading researcher in the area of relationships and conflict management, and his primary focus has been marital conflict. He has found that simply getting a couple to refocus their energy on something different for twenty minutes allows them to come back together to restart their conversation, better able to calmly discuss and start working toward solutions.[7]

When the sparks fly and conflict erupts between you and your teenager, don't allow things to spiral out of control.

The same thing can happen with your teenager! Take a time-out when you feel the argument is no longer productive and is starting to heat up. It's important to know that you're only calling a temporary break. This is not your chance to completely avoid the argument—it's merely a time to calm down before coming back together to resolve the conflict. The key is to make a commitment to resolve the conflict at a later time. A time-out that

．　．　．

doesn't eventually attempt to resolve the problem is, in reality, a withdrawal.

If you follow this rule, you'll see immediate results: fewer angry words exchanged, fewer hurt feelings, and more peaceful resolution. That's worth the effort!

7

HEALTHY HABIT #1: SET GROUND
RULES FOR FAIR FIGHTS

You play games by the rules. You drive by the rules. You even fill out your tax forms by the rules. So why do so many families look at us blankly when we tell them to fight by the rules?

Before you experience more conflict with your teenager, we encourage you to spend some time establishing rules with your family on ways to resolve future arguments. A bit of advance rule-setting concerning what is permitted and what is not could save you and your teen hours of pain during conflict resolution. It's a great idea to tackle these guidelines when tempers are calm and things are pretty good in

. . .

the relationship; it's a lot harder to work on these in the heat of the moment.

FIND FREEDOM IN RULES

While some people see rules as merely restrictive, the truth is that rules are freeing. Rules provide structure and safety. Noted psychologist Laurence Steinberg has studied parent-adolescent conflict for a number of years. He notes that to establish ground rules for conflict resolution, both the parent and the adolescent should agree to treat each other with respect and to listen to each other's point of view. The parent should provide a positive note at the beginning of the discussion by stating a desire to be fair.[8]

> Teens have a heightened sense of fairness. Point out that ground rules will promote fair play.

The key word for creating rules is *fair*. Most teens have a heightened sense of fairness. Pointing out that these ground rules will promote fair play will motivate them to help set them.

Rules for fair fighting block negative consequences of conflict from harming your family. Remember the four outcomes of poorly managed conflict we looked at in chapter 3? One rule might be to take a time-out whenever you see one of these four things developing—withdrawal, escalation, belittling, or exaggerated or false ideas. The time-out protects your family.

Another rule might be to stick to the point. In our family, that meant we could not bring past mistakes into a current argument. If God doesn't choose to remember our past transgressions (Jeremiah 31:34), who are we to use prior offenses as ammunition?

The best way to establish rules is by asking each family member: "What guidelines do we need to keep us from getting out of control or dishonoring each other when we argue?" If you need help getting started, take a look at the sidebar below and use those ideas as a jumping-off place. After your family brainstorms some rules, write them down and post them somewhere you can see them during an argument. We kept our rules for fair fighting on the refrigerator because most of our conflicts occurred at

---

RULES FOR FAIR FIGHTING

Your family will want to come up with your own set of rules, but here are a few to get you started.

- Listen to the other person and really try to understand.
- Don't resort to yelling, verbal threats, name calling, or abuse.
- Keep a respectful and loving atmosphere.
- Don't interrupt.
- Don't walk away unless both sides have agreed to a time-out.
- Stick to the issue at hand.
- Avoid saying "never" or "always."
- Avoid defensiveness.
- Be truthful.
- Fight to resolve the issue, not to win.

．　．　．

family mealtimes while we were eating in the kitchen.

Start simple. Most parents and teens can't remember too many rules when they are in the heat of an argument. But having something in writing that you can fall back on will tend to calm the emotions. The calmer the argument, the better chance you'll have of reaching an outcome that honors and respects all the participants. Researchers have even discovered that the first thirty seconds of a disagreement can determine the next two hours of arguing—whether it will be in honor or in anger.

Dads especially need the safety of rules and calmness to finish a fight in a healthy manner. If the rules for fighting are not clear and a man feels overwhelmed by angry words, his tendency will be to withdraw. As we have previously discussed, it's the withdrawal that can do such damage.

Once the rules are in place, you've got a reference point. When you realize that one or both of you is pushing those limits, it's time for that time-out!

8

HEALTHY HABIT #2: LUV TALK
AND WIN/WIN SOLUTIONS

Since conflicts are inevitable in these years as your child is maturing and developing his or her own identity, they become tools a teenager utilizes to help him grow up and—eventually—leave the house as a young adult. No wonder it's so important to keep those patterns of handling conflict moving in a healthy direction! You're helping to establish patterns that will last your child an adult lifetime.

Developing healthy habits in your relationship is not as complicated as you think. You'll find that the simplest changes bring dramatic improvements. And the healthiest habit you can develop is to focus on loving communication with your teen. In our counseling practice, we like to help parents adopt a helpful communication method we call "LUV Talk." LUV Talk helps parents reach a deep understanding with their teens while building trust and promoting harmony in the home.

BIG MAC COMMUNICATION

To help you understand what LUV Talk is, we want to ask you a very important question. Have you ever used the drive-through at McDonald's? This might sound odd, but you'd be surprised how similar making an order at your local McDonald's is to LUV Talk!

McDonald's has spent millions of dollars researching how to create an experience for their customers that will keep them coming back. They want to be sure that their customers have a satisfying experience when ordering and eating at McDonald's. They appreciate the fact that if a customer is unsatisfied with any part of her experience, the customer may not return, thus costing the franchise lots of money. This is why McDonald's communicates with you the way they do.

When you place an order at the drive-through, what happens? First, the attendant asks what you would like to order; then you give your order. What happens next is the crucial part of your communication with the attendant and the reason McDonald's keeps its customers satisfied. The attendant repeats back your order.

For example, you say, "I would like a Big Mac, large fries, and a Diet Coke," and the attendant repeats back, "You ordered a Big Mac, large fries, and a Diet Coke. Would you like anything else with that order?" This is your opportunity to add more to your order because you just got a craving for an Oreo McFlurry, or you correct the order because the attendant repeated it back wrong.

Big Mac Communication is the essence of LUV Talk. It's as simple as ordering lunch at McDonald's!

Imagine what would happen if you made your order of a Big Mac, large fries, and a Diet Coke, and the attendant poked his head out the window and stared you down for a moment. You'd feel pretty awkward, right? Then let's say the voice came back over the intercom and said, "You know, I was just looking at you and I think the Big Mac and large fries would not be a good idea. You look really overweight, so maybe the McSalad would be a better choice." How would you respond? "You know, I am so glad you pointed out my weight problem. That means so much to me. I think I will have that McSalad."

Sound realistic? I doubt it! You'd probably have a few choice words to let the attendant know just what you thought of him and his opinion! You'd steer clear of any fast-food restaurant where the employees were permitted to treat you that way.

But parents have the potential to treat their teenagers with the same insensitivity. When a teen comes to her parents with her "order" of feelings and needs, sometimes a parent responds, "Oh come on, I can't believe you feel that way! Don't take it so seriously. You're misinterpreting what I said!" or "You're too sensitive!" Don't you think that teen will think twice before she offers that parent her "order" of needs and feelings a second time? She'll look elsewhere for support and hope she can find it—somewhere.

Here's a reality: Your teenager has individual feelings and individual needs that are different from yours! Too often we try to mold our teens into what we think they should be instead of allowing them to work out the person God is molding them to become. When we try to force our teens toward ideas and personality traits that are way outside their thinking or person, conflicts will erupt. Then, amazingly enough, we wonder why they are unhappy or dissatisfied with us.

LUV TALK

Before we give you the details of how LUV Talk works, we need to explain the fundamental truth surrounding this method of communication, found in James 1:19: "Be quick to listen, slow to speak, and slow to get angry." The Bible is full of many truths, but isn't this verse incredible? It is the road map to healthy communication and the essence of LUV Talk.

Here is how LUV Talk works on a practical level. Take the McDonald's metaphor. When a misunderstanding develops with another person, think of yourselves as customer and employee. This distinction is crucial—remember, the customer has his own set of rules to follow during the discussion and the employee does too. We encourage you to use some sort of object to signify who the customer is. (For example, the "customer" can wear a hat or hold a pen. When you change places and the customer becomes the "employee," the object goes to the new customer.)

> **LUV is an acronym that stands for *Listen, Understand,* and *Validate.***

We recommend that the person with the most pressing grievance be the first customer. This is often the teenager.

The customer has three major rules to follow when giving an order. These rules keep the discussion focused and the conflict structured, which allows the customer to feel understood.

Customer rule #1: Speak with "I" statements.
There's a big difference between "I get upset when we're late" and "You always make me late!" Too often in conflict we start playing the blame game. "You"

this and "you" that permeate the conversation to the point that the employee or listener can no longer do her job because she is too busy defending herself. So talk about your own side of things.

Customer rule #2: Make your "I" statements share your feelings and needs.

Sticking with just feelings and needs also helps prevent you from blaming, which is so destructive when trying to resolve your conflicts. Practically, if your teen was speaking first, this might look like: "When I don't get my allowance on time, I get frustrated, and I need there to be a system in place to ensure that I get my allowance every week."

This rule keeps the conflict from escalating out of control by allowing the customer to verbally express his feelings and needs and thereby gain a true understanding of them. The key is the ability to discuss them in safety.

Customer rule #3: Keep it short and concise.

As you'll see in a minute, the "employee" in this discussion eventually has to repeat back what the customer is saying. If you make a thirty-minute doctrinal statement, the employee will get overwhelmed and won't be able to process or understand the order. Also, too many words can become tedious, making you lose the employee's attention.

The heart of LUV Talk—the very *essence* of LUV Talk—is found in the rules for the employee. LUV is actually an acronym that stands for *Listen, Understand,* and *Validate.* These three fundamental principles must be followed in order for resolution to occur through conflict.

Employee rule #1: "L" is for Listen.

The most fundamental aspect of listening is repeating back what your teenager says. Why? Because if you can repeat back your teen's words and concerns, you prove to him or her that you're really paying attention. Remember, your teenager is the customer and is supposed to describe feelings and needs in short, bite-sized pieces. The employee's job is to repeat back what the customer is saying, just like in the drive-through. When the employee repeats back what the customer has ordered, the customer gets the chance to correct the order. So if you aren't listening and really understanding what your teen said, your teen will know—and will have a chance to point that out.

Employee rule #2: "U" is for Understand.

The second job of the employee is to seek understanding. We do this by asking questions. If you are confused by what your teenager is saying, or if you feel as if something is missing, all you have to do is ask. Unfortunately, in the heat of battle we tend not to ask questions that promote understanding, so this takes a bit of effort! LUV Talk provides a structure that helps you keep calm and think rationally, which allows for the questions that will really help you reach understanding.

Questions can also be helpful during the repeating-back phase. "So what I hear you saying is that you get frustrated when I forget to give you your allowance. But can I ask a question? I don't think I completely understand just how frustrated you are. Can you rate your frustration from 1 to 10?" Questions allow you to dig deeper into your communication with your teen . . . to unravel the mystery surrounding conflict . . . to gain answers!

Employee rule #3: "V" is for Validate.

Now we come to the most important part of the employee's job description: validation. Simply put, validation is allowing your teenager to be an individual, to have separate feelings and needs from those of your own. You invalidate your teenager by putting your own thoughts and feelings onto her and not allowing her to be an individual. Validation says something more like, "I'm sorry I hurt your feelings; how can I make it right?" It is not evaluating what your teenager believes or feels, but rather accepting it.

Validation can become tricky. There are times when you offend your teenager simply because she has misunderstood what you said. When a teen responds by accusing you of something you certainly didn't mean to do, it's easy to get caught up in the details of that accusation and lose sight of what's more important: her feelings. You can learn to say, "I am so sorry for hurting your feelings. That was not my intention, but obviously I did hurt you, so how can I make it right?" That's the way to validate a teenager's feelings!

DAD AND GREG'S EXCELLENT COMMUNICATION ADVENTURE

Now it's time to show you LUV Talk in action. Let's take a look at an event from the Smalley family files. . . .

One day, while driving in northern California, our

family became very tired and irritable. After a family vote we all—Dad, Mom, Michael, Kari, and me—decided to stretch our legs. Up the road a few miles, we found a beautiful river that had a special surprise.

As we were exploring the river, I (Greg) discovered that moss had formed over the rocks, creating a very slick river bottom. What was even more amazing was that the water had carved out a natural slide. However, there was one minor problem. As you slid down, unless you landed in a small pool, you were in danger of going over a waterfall.

After several practice runs we determined that you could slide about ten yards and still make it into the landing pool. We were having a relaxing time until Dad showed up. Watching us slide down the river, he felt this would make a great picture. Having never met a camera I didn't like, I enthusiastically volunteered to go first. However, somehow Dad talked me into starting at the very top. Looking down at the steep slide, I realized that it would be difficult to stop in the landing pool. As he attempted to persuade me, Dad said something that would eventually cause me much pain. "Trust me. You'll do fine. If you don't hit the pool, I'll stop you!"

As he got into position, I pushed off and went racing down the slide. Suddenly, I hit a bump and flew off course. Instantly I passed my father—who was still trying to take the picture—and headed straight for the waterfall.

As I went over the falls, I tried to push off to keep my balance. Unfortunately, I kicked too hard and landed flat on my back. *Slapppp!* The sound of my back flop echoed throughout the canyon. As I struggled toward the riverbank, my father's words, "Trust me . . . I'll stop you!" haunted me. When he appeared at the top of the falls, I started to scream at him but quickly stopped. Watching my mother race down the trail was like watching a mother bear rear up to attack the person who had wounded her cub. It was awesome! I didn't know my mom could move that fast. Through this experience, it was my sensitive mom who was shaken up the most. In fact, this was one time in her life when if she could have reached Dad, there's no telling what she would have done to him!

After the disaster at the waterfall, my dad and I (Greg) could have used LUV Talk to discuss the situation. If I had been the customer, first I could

> *The Lord is merciful and gracious; he is slow to get angry and full of unfailing love.*
> *He will not constantly accuse us, nor remain angry forever.*
> *He has not punished us for all our sins, nor does he deal with us as we deserve.*
> *For his unfailing love toward those who fear him is as great as the height of the heavens above the earth.*
> *He has removed our rebellious acts as far away from us as the east is from the west.*
>
> PSALM 103:8-12

63

have started by saying something like, "I feel frustrated when you try to talk me into things that you aren't sure about." He then would have repeated back what I said. "I hear you saying that it's frustrating when I talk you into doing things when I have no idea how it's going to turn out." Yes!

I might have continued with, "I feel hurt because it seemed like you were more interested in taking a 'fun' picture than making sure I was safe." He might have said in response, "It sounds like I hurt your feelings because I was more focused on taking a picture than on your safety." Yes!

Once I shared all my feelings and/or needs, then we could switch places, with Dad becoming the customer. Dad might have said, "I truly believed that taking a picture of you sliding down the river was completely safe." I'd respond, "I hear you saying that you thought I'd be safe." Yes!

"I felt that if there was any danger, I'd be able to stop you."

"So you're saying that you believed you could stop me if there was a problem." Yes!

"I felt extremely scared when I realized you were going over the edge." And so on . . .

Do you get point? The process is simply one person sharing his feelings or needs and the other person repeating back what he heard. If the person repeats it back wrong, you don't panic. You simply restate what you said. Then when one person finishes expressing his feelings and needs, you trade places. This process goes on until both feel listened to, understood, and validated. It's that simple.

WIN/WIN SOLUTIONS

Once you've listened, understood, and validated each other, you are ready to solve the original problem. Throw out any idea of a win/lose arrangement and pursue only win/win solutions—ones that you reach mutually.

Brainstorm all the possible solutions for your conflict. This time is meant to be creative and not critical. There is no such thing as a bad idea during the brainstorming session. If either of you begins to evaluate or criticize a possible solution, you might find yourselves right back in the middle of a heated conflict. Let the goofy ideas fly free—you never know when one might lead to a win/win idea!

Let's go back to the allowance issue and see how this could work. A win/lose solution might be for your teenager to raid your purse or wallet if you forget to dole out the allowance. But win/win solutions could include marking "allowance time" on the calendar, setting an alarm on the computer or handheld, setting aside time for a regularly scheduled "date"

. . .

with your teen to talk about the week and give out the allowance, or even setting up a direct deposit from the parent's checking account to the teen's.

After you come up with all the possible solutions to your conflict, it's time to start evaluating them and to pick a solution that works for both of you. Once you agree on a solution, live with it for a while and then come back together and reevaluate it.

- **Is it working for everyone involved?** Maybe you've tried marking it on the calendar but you've still forgotten two out of three times. Guess what? That's not working for your teen, so it's time for a new solution.
- **Could it be improved?** Maybe you've set up the regular "dates" with your teen but realize you like them so much you want to have one every week instead of just twice a month!

You need to force yourselves to evaluate your solutions because this will allow you the opportunity to adapt the solution if your first idea is not working just the way you hoped. Relationships are dynamic and are continuously changing with the tides of emotions and circumstances that present themselves in our lives, so sometimes solutions need to be reevaluated or replaced.

· · ·

Finally, if after using the above steps, the conflict has not ended and a "win/win" solution is not reached, then you either need to repeat the process or seek a third party to help bring about an honorable resolution.

CALL FOR HELP!

Everyone knows to call 911 in the event of an emergency. But does your family have a plan for the event of a relationship emergency? When LUV Talk and problem-solving break down, you need to call for help.

Ahead of time—before you've reached a major impasse, if possible—identify a person you both agree on who could listen to both sides and run interference. Obviously you won't want to drag outsiders into your private difficulties unless both you and your teen agree that this person could be a helpful referee or solution finder. This person needs to be able to maintain unbiased opinions, be someone you both respect and feel safe with, and maintain confidentiality and privacy. A grandparent could fit this bill, if he or she remains objective. An older friend from church, a pastor or youth pastor, a professional counselor— there are many people willing and available to be a listening ear for you and your teen.

Having someone to help resolve major conflicts does several important things for your family. First, it provides support and accountability. A genuine friend sticks with you through difficult times and provides the necessary accountability to resolve the problem. In the Bible, we read that we should "share each other's troubles and problems, and in this way obey the law of Christ" (Galatians 6:2). Secondly, when you get an outside opinion to help solve the conflict, you could just be tapping into a wealth of new information or perspectives you hadn't considered before. This, too, is scriptural: "Two people can accomplish more than twice as much as one; they get a better return for their labor" (Ecclesiastes 4:9). It might be the new material that helps you and your teenager come to an agreement.

MAJOR ON THE MAJORS . . . MINOR ON THE MINORS!

Not every problem between you and your teen is going to call for formal Big Mac Communication, although the LUV principles of listening, understanding, and validating are habits that should infiltrate all interactions in your family as much as possible. There are problems—lots of them—that could be considered "minor" ones.

Between you and your teenager, take the time to rate the severity of the conflict and the difficulty of the problem solving involved. You could use the 0-10 scale, with 10 being a major issue. If a conflict is judged to be between 1 and 5, then you may not need to use all of the steps to reach a "win/win" solution. But if you assign between a 6 and 10 to a particular issue, then you need to be careful. Agree on the number that signals the need for careful attention.

The reason we caution you about "major" versus "minor" issues is that teenagers need the freedom to start making some of their own choices. But this is a process. The moment a child becomes an adolescent, you're not going to allow her the total freedom to make every decision. Like anything else, your teens need to earn the right to make decisions. Depending upon the age and maturity level, which will differ for every child, a teenager needs to have the opportunity to put into practice all the things that he's been taught. Of course, your teen will have to earn increased responsibility in terms of making decisions, but you must at least give him the opportunity to prove he can make wise decisions.

> *Dear children, let us stop just saying we love each other; let us really show it by our actions.*
>
> 1 JOHN 3:18

QUICK, SLOW, SLOW

Remember the verse we plucked from the book of James? "Be quick to listen, slow to speak, and slow to get angry" (1:19). It's been said that God gave us two ears and only one mouth so we'd listen twice as much as we speak! If your teenager is in the mood to talk, capitalize on that and listen, listen, listen! And LUV him—listen, understand, validate.

Ever heard this little rhyme?

> *A wise old owl sat on an oak,*
> *The more he saw the less he spoke;*
> *The less he spoke the more he heard;*
> *Why aren't we like that wise old bird?*

Big Mac Communication . . . LUV Talk . . . wise old owls . . . there are many ways to approach communicating with your teen, even during times when you're not at loggerheads over issues. But all of them involve putting aside your own agenda in order to love and meet another's needs. That's the essence of parenting—and the essence of following Jesus! It's not easy, but when you do it, with God's help, the results will be phenomenal.

HEALTHY HABIT #3: THE FREEDOM OF NATURAL CONSEQUENCES

Teenagers need the opportunity to make decisions. As they move closer to adulthood, the stakes grow higher. In their preschool years, the biggest choices they made were what flavor of ice cream to get in their cone, whether to paint or play make-believe, and whether or not to share their favorite toy with their best friend. But with each passing year, the choices mount—and so does the difficulty of those choices. Teens are just a few years away from needing to decide things as major as whom they will marry and what career they will pursue. How can they prepare for decisions this life changing and with such long-term consequences?

· · ·

As parents, you can help your teens not only by giving them chances to choose for themselves, but also by holding them accountable for their choices. If they make poor choices, they need to be held accountable to face the logical and natural consequences that follow. Check out a few examples of how this works.

PAINFUL CONSEQUENCES

It was 12:00 A.M. and I (Michael) was nowhere to be found. My parents called my girlfriend's house to see if I had left yet, and she confirmed that I had left about twenty minutes earlier. Now the worrying set in. "What if" questions flooded my parents' consciousness like a roaring river, overwhelming their thoughts until they finally released the situation to God.

You can imagine their relief when I finally walked in the front door. (I should have probably chosen the *back* door with the amount of anxiety my parents were experiencing.) I then boldly announced the reason for my tardiness: a speeding ticket. The tension mounted exponentially.

"I know you warned me about speeding, but—" I started in immediately. I was already beginning to mount my defense. But to my surprise, neither my dad nor my mom reacted. What they did next helped me and them as well.

• • •

They could have lit into me, scolding me for being irresponsible and careless. This only would have caused me to get more defensive, maybe triggering a full-scale shouting match. What would have been the results? We would have felt less secure in our relationship. My parents' relationship might have suffered as a result of the anxiety and conflict.

But my parents made a smarter decision: They didn't react to my speeding ticket. Why not? They didn't need to!

Some of you out there might be thinking that our parents were being irresponsible by not disciplining me for this transgression. That is the beauty of natural consequences. We as parents don't always have to discipline our children. Life itself can be a great disciplinarian!

I had already suffered through the fear of returning home with a speeding ticket and not knowing what was going to happen to me when my parents found out. The officer who gave the ticket scared me more than my parents ever could. If only parents could use those incredible lights and siren when they approached their children to discipline them!

Besides the embarrassment of getting the ticket, I also learned how much tickets cost. Not only did I have to pay that fine, I also had to pay for the rise in my insurance coverage cost and for the classes I needed to take to get the ticket removed from my driving record. When you added it all up, I doled out some $200 for my speeding ticket. At that time of my life, the pinch in my cash flow hurt me much more than anything my parents could have imposed upon me.

NATURAL CONSEQUENCES

"Natural and logical consequences teach children to learn from the situation, thus encouraging self-control and self-discipline," writes Shirley King in the *Boise Family* magazine.[9] Natural consequences allow children to make mistakes on their own, free from parental involvement. Using this technique means letting the world and the effects of your teenager's decisions serve as discipline.

Natural consequences are not about control. When we are fearful of our teenagers making mistakes and either severely harming themselves or embarrassing us, we might compensate for that fear with control. Control makes us feel like things are not as bad as they are. In other words, control gives us a false sense of security.

When you start trying to control your teenager, watch out! That only causes problems. When you give her something to rebel against, she will almost certainly rebel.

If teens don't get a chance to flex their decision-making muscles, how will they be ready for that big, scary adult world out there? It's a parent's greatest challenge to help his or her young people learn to think for themselves—and to learn to think *wisely!* And that means giving them the opportunity to shape their own time and choices. It also means giving them the chance to deal with their own consequences—without bailing them out.

Think about it: Wouldn't it be better to let your teen make a few mistakes in decision making now, when his choices are still minor-league ones and he's still under your supervision, than to send him unprepared into the world of adult choices and have him make his first poor choices there?

> **Provide love and support for your children when they suffer the consequences of their choices.**

Try to picture this decision-making process as great life practice. The more opportunities you provide for your teen to make choices on her own, the better she'll become at making right choices. When a bad choice is made, it hurts—we all know this principle too well. No one likes to hurt, especially not teenagers. Therefore, you'll find that your teen will do whatever she can to avoid making poor decisions if she knows the consequences of those decisions will be painful.

Let's look at an example. If your fourteen-year-old decides not to go to basketball practice one week,

. . .

what happens? She doesn't improve her skills, her teammates get mad at her, and she probably won't play in the game on Saturday night. Those are tough consequences for a fourteen-year-old. But in terms of life-changing consequences, that result is far better than if she were to make the same choice at age twenty and lose her college basketball scholarship.

Natural consequences are important because they allow your teenagers to take responsibility for themselves. Behavioral training—rewards and punishments—can only go so far when it comes to teaching our kids to take responsibility. This approach is popular because of its relatively quick results with children. However, behavioral methods merely train children to do what's right, rather than teaching them *why* they should do what is right. It is that "why" that's most important for children—and especially teenagers—to learn. The "why" leads to responsibility.

HAVE NO FEAR

An English philosopher named F. H. Bradley has written, "The man who has ceased to fear has ceased to care."[10] What a great quote! Fear, at times, is mind numbing. And many parents of teenagers have to struggle with and deal with fears. It's a scary proposition to let go of some of the control we've been able to exercise over our children, partly because it has been all about protecting them. (Or, if we're honest, it's sometimes been about making ourselves look good as parents.) Now that they're teenagers wanting to exercise their freedom, parents often let go with fear and trepidation. In our counseling practice, we've often had clients protest, "But you're asking us just to let them get hurt!"

Fear is the single biggest obstacle hindering the system of natural consequences. It's fear of letting go of the control that helps soothe our worrying minds. Fear of realizing that our teenagers are going to make mistakes, some potentially big. Fear that our teenagers will reject us when we don't step in on occasion to help them when they need it.

These are all legitimate fears. Like the quote, these fears show how much we care for our children. We care about making the right choices as parents. We care about the future well-being of our children. We care that our children don't grow up to be irresponsible adults. And because we care, we accept the fact that fear is part of caring, and we move ahead anyway to let our children make decisions and live with the natural consequences of their choices. This is a part of our parenting style.

The first major step in implementing natural consequences is to *not let your fears prevent you from doing*

what is best—in the long-term—for your teenager.
Even though fear can show how much we care for our
children, it does have another side. Fear's downside
rears its ugly head each time we become too unbal-
anced, allowing our worries rather than sound judg-
ment to influence our choices.

The second important principle in making natural
consequences work in your home is to *be encouraging*. If you ridicule your teenagers for making mistakes, they'll simply learn to resent you as parents.
Provide love and support for your children when they
suffer the consequences of their choices.

Learning the hard way
I can think of one time I (Michael) was determined to
be the hero of a very important skit being performed
at a summer camp. I know now that my parents were
not fond of the idea of what I had to do in the skit,
but they allowed me to make the decision for myself.

At the closing of camp, all the kids and their families gathered around the pool for a grand finale. Non-
stop action best describes what the skit was about.
We had people flying all over the equipment at the
main pool for the pure enjoyment of the crowd. Much
of the action was actually quite dangerous, and the
job I chose was especially risky.

Yes, I allowed my masculine absurdity to get in the

way of good sound thinking. I'd chosen to perform the skit-ending dive off the high dive of the pool, which was about fifteen feet high. Of course, diving off the high dive might not sound too crazy, but when you're sitting in the bowl of a kayak at the time, things become a tad more dangerous.

I can remember looking at the faces in the crowd, all of them wondering exactly what I was doing sitting on the high dive in a blue kayak. As we neared the end of the skit, the crowd realized that one of the counselors was pushing me off the board while I remained in the kayak. People started erupting in cheers to see how this was going to turn out. My parents were not as enthused.

Of course, I had not actually thought about practicing this stunt, and frankly, who would? I just figured that the counselor had to push me hard enough to clear the kayak off the board. I imagined that if he didn't push hard enough, the kayak might start falling before the back end of it cleared the board. This would mean flipping upside down and falling fifteen feet to the water on my head—and landing upside down.

> *Get rid of all bitterness, rage, anger, harsh words, and slander, as well as all types of malicious behavior. Instead, be kind to each other, tenderhearted, forgiving one another, just as God through Christ has forgiven you.*
>
> EPHESIANS 4:31-32

Guess what? He didn't push hard enough! I landed so hard and awkwardly that it actually knocked the wind out of me. This didn't really matter, though, because my head was underwater and I couldn't have breathed even if I wanted to.

The impact from the fall made me drop my paddle, and I couldn't roll back over in order to breathe again. It felt like an eternity. No one thought to actually jump in the pool and flip me over. That would have taken away from the drama—the crowd was probably thinking it was all part of the act. I knew different!

My only chance of getting back over was to try a hand roll, which is basically using just your hands to flip the kayak upright. I had never been able to do this before, but considering the danger I was in of drowning in front of a thousand people, I figured now was the moment to learn.

God was with me! Somehow I managed to flip the kayak back upright. My parents had warned me of the danger of this stunt, and they could have reminded me of this fact as I gasped for air on the side of the pool. But I didn't hear any "I told you so's" from them. Instead, they hugged me!

When your teenagers make poor choices, instead of rebuking them, why not support them in their time of need? This does not mean you're condoning their actions. The message it sends your teen is, "No matter

. . .

what, we love you!" This acceptance for who they are and not what they do is extremely important in the development of responsibility.

Teenagers shouldn't become afraid to make choices in their lives for fear of rejection by their parents. They need to be free to become who they truly are.

Working with natural consequences is not a complicated set of rules and regulations. Instead, it's about letting go of control and fear, and then being encouraging and loving when your teenager goes through tough times.

. . . 10 . . .

ACHIEVE THE DREAM

Do you dream of a day when, from the peace and quiet of your empty nest, you receive a call from your adult child simply calling to report that all is well—in his spiritual life with God, in his career, in his family, in his physical health? He is calling to talk with you because, though he no longer lives in the same house, his relationship with you is still loving and close, founded on great depths of mutual regard and respect and the joy of a thousand happy memories.

If conflicts have created a negative and discouraging atmosphere in your home, that dream can feel like an impossibly hopeless fantasy. But, with God's help, that day could come for you and your teenager. We hope it will!

. . .

Get on your knees and pray for your teenager. Pray, too, over your parenting decisions and communication. Ask God for the humility to seek your child's forgiveness and get a fresh start, if that is necessary. Put LUV Talk to work, starting right now to listen, understand, and validate. See conflict as an opportunity to work things out—together.

Changes take time. So does growing up. Be persistent and consistent in your pursuit of a growing relationship with your child. Keep sending the message that you love her, even when she dyes her hair magenta, even when he wrecks the car, even when they have to endure the natural consequences of their own foolhardy early decisions. Affirm their good decisions, and keep watching the progress of their independent thinking and the improving quality of their choices. Your relationship can be launched into a new dimension during these years of launching your teen into adulthood. What a bold adventure for both parents and teens!

WEB SITES

www.christianitytoday.com/parenting—Includes articles from *Christian Parenting Today,* including a teen section, message boards, columns from child-rearing experts, and even a prayer network.

www.familyresources.net—Offers resources to help families in the many aspects of their daily lives including marriage, parenting, financial matters, spiritual growth, health and fitness, and entertainment.

www.parentsoup.com/teens—This site, part of www.ivillage.com, includes articles on topics such as education, discipline, dealing with bullies, talking to your teen about dating, and much more. Also includes message boards, articles from parenting experts, and recommended resources.

www.smalleyonline.com—SmalleyOnline can help you achieve lifetime intimacy in all your most important relationships. Our site is dedicated to providing you the best in on-line relationship enrichment by offering articles, relationship Q & A, and on-line registration to our live events.

CLINICAL RESOURCES

www.meiernewlifeclinics.com—Meier New Life Clinics provide family and individual counseling with a team of Christian therapists. Check out their Web site for more information, including who might benefit from therapy, and for clinic locations.

． ． ．

www.smalleyonline.com—Struggling with how to parent
effectively and consistently? Wondering how to be a
better stepparent? Not sure where to find a Christian
counselor in your area or how to find the time to meet
with one? Our counselors and psychologists are available
to consult with you over the phone. Our staff can help
educate you on the skills and knowledge necessary to
be the best parent you can be. Check out our Web site
or call (417) 335-5882.

SEMINARS AND CURRICULUM

Homes of Honor parenting series. Parents can better
learn how to raise their children when they can discuss
their strengths and weaknesses with other parents. This
series, available from www.smalleyonline.com, has eight
sessions with over four hours of teaching by Gary Smalley.
This set includes a participant's workbook plus a copy of
the best-selling book *The Key to Your Child's Heart*. May
also be used with small groups.

BOOKS

On Parenting
Adolescence Isn't Terminal by Dr. Kevin Leman

The Art of Talking with Your Teenager by Paul W. Swets

Bound by Honor by Gary and Greg Smalley. Provides
parents with the keys to building a great relationship
with their teenager and preparing him or her for life as
a successful Christian adult. Focuses on the crucial need
to increase honor in the home.

Helping the Struggling Adolescent by Dr. Les Parrott III

How to Really Love Your Teenager by Ross Campbell

Leaving the Light On by Dr. Gary Smalley and Dr. John Trent

Life on the Edge by Dr. James Dobson

LifeTraining by Dr. Joe White

Parenting Adolescents by Kevin Huggins

Parenting Teens by Dr. Bruce Narramore and Vern C. Lewis

Parenting Teens with Love & Logic by Foster W. Cline, M.D. and Jim Fay. Love means giving your teens opportunities to be responsible and empowering them to make their own decisions. Logic means allowing them to live with the natural consequences of their mistakes and showing empathy for the pain they will experience.

Parents' Guide to Teen Health by Focus on the Family

Suddenly They're 13 by David and Claudia Arp

Toughlove by Phyllis and David York and Ted Wachtel

On Dealing with Divorce
The Fresh Start Divorce Recovery Workbook by Bob Burns and Tom Whiteman

Helping Children Survive Divorce by Dr. Archibald D. Hart

Life after Divorce by Bobbie Reed, Ph.D.

On Blended Families
Blended Families by Maxine Marsolini

Devotions for Couples in Blended Families: Living and Loving in a New Family by Margaret Smith-Broersma

On Career Counseling
The Career Counselor by Les and Leslie Parrot

What Color Is Your Parachute? by Richard Nelson Bolles

. . .

For Teens
7 Habits of Highly Effective Teens by Sean Covey. Provides a step-by-step guide to help teens improve self-image, build friendships, resist peer pressure, achieve their goals, get along with their parents, and much more.

. . . ENDNOTES . . .

1 P. F. Rice, *The Adolescent: Development, Relationships, and Culture*, 6th ed. (Needham Heights, Mass.: Allyn and Bacon, 1990), 428.

2 S. B. Silverberg and L. Steinberg, "Adolescent Autonomy, Parent-Adolescent Conflict, and Parental Well-Being," *Journal of Youth and Adolescence,* 16 (1987), 293–312.

3 R. Larson and M. H. Richards, "Daily Companionship in Late Childhood and Early Adolescence: Changing Developmental Contexts," *Child Development,* 62 (1991), 284–300.

4 N. A. Sprinthall and W. A. Collins, *Adolescent Psychology: A Developmental View* (New York: McGraw-Hill, Inc., 1995), 246.

5 C. S. Lewis, *The Last Battle* (New York: Collier Books, 1970), 136.

6 John Gottman, *Why Marriages Succeed or Fail* (New York: Simon and Schuster, 1994), 173.

7 Ibid., 177-178.

8 L. Steinberg and A. Levine, *You and Your Adolescent* (New York: Harper Perennial, 1990), 35–36.

9 Shirley King, "Democratic Parenting: Finding a Balance between Punitive and Permissive,"*Boise Family*.

10 F. H. Bradley (1846-1924), English philosopher, *Aphorisms,* no. 63 (1930).

Marriage Alive International, Inc., founded by husband-wife team Claudia and David Arp, MSW, is a nonprofit marriage- and family-enrichment ministry dedicated to providing resources, seminars, and training to empower churches to help build better marriages and families. The Arps are marriage and family educators, popular speakers, award-winning authors, and frequent contributors to print and broadcast media. They have appeared as marriage experts on programs such as *Today, CBS This Morning,* and *Focus on the Family.* Their Marriage Alive seminar is in great demand across the U.S. and in Europe.

The Mission of Marriage Alive is to identify, train, and empower leaders who invest in others by building strong marriage and family relationships through the integration of biblical truth, contemporary research, practical application, and fun.

Our Resources and Services
- Marriage and family books and small-group resources
- Video-based educational programs including *10 Great Dates to Energize Your Marriage* and *Second Half of Marriage*
- Marriage, pre-marriage, and parenting seminars, including *Before You Say "I Do," Marriage Alive, Second Half of Marriage,* and *Empty Nesting*
- Coaching, mentoring, consulting, training, and leadership development

CONTACT MARRIAGE ALIVE INTERNATIONAL AT WWW.MARRIAGEALIVE.COM OR (888) 690-6667.

The Smalley Relationship Center, founded by Dr. Gary Smalley, offers many varied resources to help people strengthen their marriage and family relationships. The Center provides marriage enrichment products, conferences, training material, articles, and clinical services—all designed to make your most important relationships *successful* relationships.

The Mission of the Smalley Relationship Center is to increase marriage satisfaction and lower the divorce rate by providing a deeper level of care. We want to help couples build strong, successful, and satisfying marriages.

Resources and Services:

- Nationwide conferences: Love Is a Decision, Marriage for a Lifetime
- Counseling services: Couples Intensive program, phone counseling
- Video series, including *Keys to Loving Relationships, Homes of Honor,* and *Secrets to Lasting Love*
- Small group leadership guide
- Articles on marriage, parenting, and stepfamilies
- Smalley Counseling Center provides counseling, national intensives, and more for couples in crisis

CONTACT SMALLEY RELATIONSHIP CENTER AT WWW.SMALLEYONLINE.COM OR 1-800-84-TODAY.